THE MAD

HOW NOT TO DO IT

APS — DISTRICT MEDIA SERVICES

ALBUQUERQUE PUBLIC SCHOOLS

INTRODUCTION

How does one write an introduction to a "How Not To Book"? The author of this book, Mr. Paul Peter Porges, had the best method. Instead of writing the introduction himself, he got somebody else to do it. It wasn't easy. He started off at the top, with the Publisher of MAD, Bill Gaines. Gaines refused. In fact he threw Porges out of his office. Porges then knocked on Editor Al Feldstein's door. Al wouldn't let him in. Besides, Al was too busy writing introductions for six other paperback MAD books and couldn't find time. Next, Porges tried Nick Meglin, the Associate Editor. But since Meglin insisted on the Movie Rights to any introduction he wrote, Porges backed off. Next was Jerry DeFuccio of the Editorial Staff. Jerry was glad to consider the idea, but only if he could pass the job along to a cocktail waitress in Bangkok, Thailand, to write-up as a term paper in her "Improve-Your-English-By-Mail" course (which Jerry was giving).

So that left me, John Putnam, Art Director of MAD. I accepted the job, reluctantly. What else could I do? As soon as Porges was out of sight, I handed the job over to Len Brenner, my Associate in the Art Department. Len threatened to quit.

So here I go with the introduction. Perhaps I should follow the instructional tone of the rest of this book and show the reader how he can avoid making a fool of himself if any friend of *his* asks him to write an introduction to a "How Not To Book."

1. Even though you are writing for a low level of intelligence (who but a near-moron would buy a book like this), you must try to avoid the kind of primer style that insults the reader with:

"...this is a book. A nice book. It is a book that starts with an in-tro-duc-tion. Do you know what an in-tro-duc-tion is? Schmuck, you're reading one right now! THIS is an in-tro-duc-tion, you pin-head!"

2. And while there is a remote chance that a genuine intellectual might pick up this book, there's no need to cater to his snobbery, so avoid stuff that goes like:

"...the arcane parameters of sub-cultures implicit in folkloric utterances as expressed in the kitsch artifacts exemplified by MAD inevitably lead to..."

3. Many Intro writers attempt the practical, "What's-In-It-For-Me?" kind of approach, but you should avoid things like:

"...and what's more, this dandy little book contains exactly one hundred-and-eighty-five funny pictures, just think of it, a laugh a minute, because, folks, it takes about one minute to look at each gag, absorb it, laugh, recover and go on the next page. And some of the gags will leave you laughing for as long as a minute and a HALF. And one gag, I forget on which page it is, will leave you doubled up on the floor for an hour, and when you consider that it only takes about thirty minutes to skim your way through most paperback humor books, you're already way ahead…"

4. The "I Knew Him When" introduction is deadly. Avoid at all costs intros that begin:

"…I was just about ready to go over the hill and desert from the Marine Corps. Boot Camp was hell. That evening in the mess hall, everyone was literally puking up the slop they were forcing us to eat, everyone, that is, but the little stranger next to me who was gobbling it up like it was gourmet food. Little did I know then, that such a greedy little oaf would one day become the author of this book…"

5. Don't forget the Stab-In-The-Back intro. You really hate the guy who asked you to write his intro but it has to sound like you have always loved him. Since, as a good hater this is almost an impossible task, avoid it as it may come out like:

"…strangely enough, Porges is funny." To *some* people. At least he assures me that there are quite a few people who think he is funny. "I tell a joke… they laugh," Porges says, with a faraway look in his eyes that fools nobody…

6. Then we have the apologetic intro. Try to avoid this one because it will inevitably end up like this:

"…that Porges! Is he ever FUN-ny!! Ya hadda *be* there!"

* * * *

So by now, you should have a good idea of How Not To Write An Introduction to a "How Not To Book." And as this brings us to the end of the Introduction, you can now go on to the rest of the book and find out how NOT to do almost anything, but then again:

Some people never learn!

John Putnam

CONTENTS

HOW NOT TO MAKE FRIENDS!

Make yourself comfortable...wherever you are!

8

Have a hot Italian sausage Pizza, with onions and anchovies, before a heavy Date.

Spike the fruit punch of a sweet-sixteen party with Polish Vodka.

Offer a broken chair to an old lady!

Insist on knowing a shortcut... and tell the driver that he doesn't know how to follow instructions!

Invent descriptive nicknames for your friends!

Blow smoke rings at an asthmatic!

Give away the gagline to someone's best joke!

During a dramatic performance, loudly tell what happened to you at the supermarket checkout counter!

16

Insist that everybody has to like your pet!

Begin conversations with: "I told you so!"

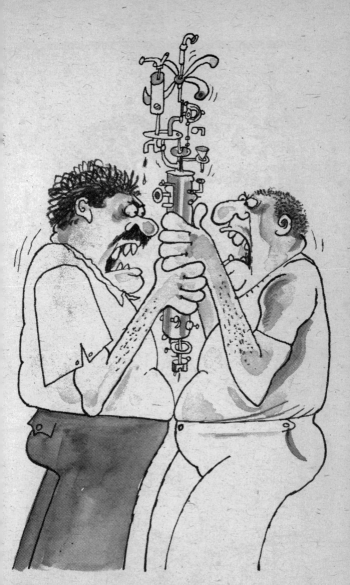

Borrow things without asking and insist they belong to you!

Read over people's shoulders...aloud!

Pick and taste from everybody's plate.

Use your Hostess's priceless Dresden plate for an ashtray!

Don't dress for the occasion!

Embrace a new health fad and try to convert everybody else to it!

Backslap your carpenter... while he has nails in his mouth.

Give practical joke gifts on important occasions!

Show an expert how the job is done!

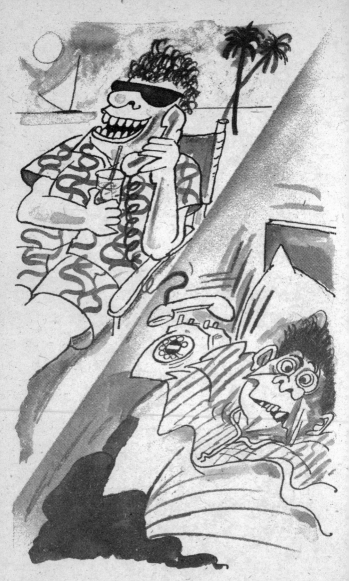

Make long distance calls without considering Time Zones!

CLASSIC
BLUNDERS

While driving with your seatbelt on.

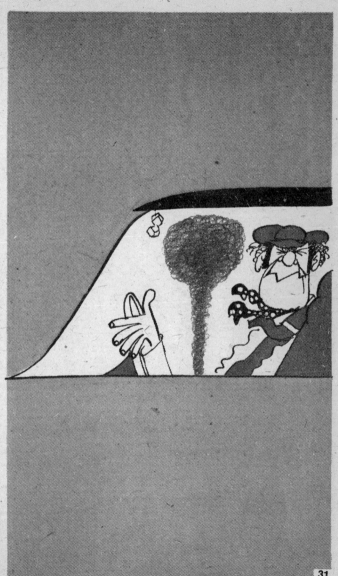

Having a passionate romance....

In a canoe.

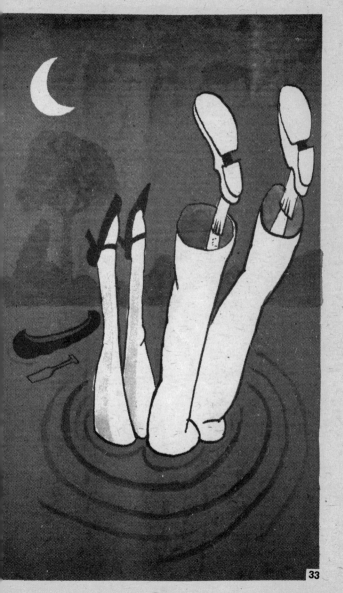

Bringing flowers....

To a hay fever sufferer.

Gas leak.

Body surfing....

At low tide!

When you were invited for the 7th at 8PM.

41

That was sitting down!

Returning from vacation....

And finding you left the refrigerator on defrost!

Tossing a salad. . . .

Next to a drafty window.

Picking up the morning paper....

Without your keys!

For the wrong bird!

Repairing a flat....

Kissing a baby....

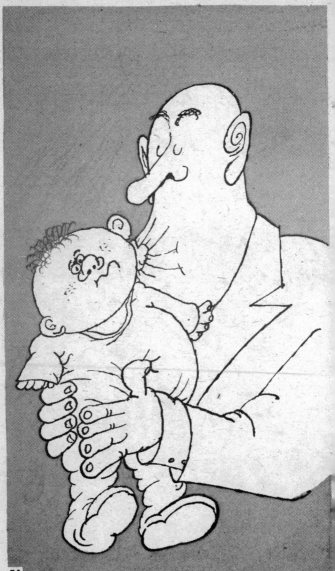

Cementing your sidewalk....

The day of the big marathon!

Repainting the toilet seat....

Without telling anyone!

THE KLUTZ

A Klutz should not climb into confining spaces with his mouth full. **60**

MAD BADGES FOR FAILURES, LOSERS

(and other personal shortcomings)

COMPULSIVE EATER

HOLIER - THAN - THOU

TEDIOUS SHOWOFF

LOUSY COOK

LOUSY DANCER

CLUMSY FIXER

CheapSkate

BAD BREATH

LOUD DRESSER

SHORT TEMPER

THE KLUTZ

A Klutz should not keep his car locked when strolling through a wild game preserve.

MISTER
HOW-NOT-TO-FIX-IT
ANSWERS
AND
QUESTIONS

Q.—We have a Cliff House smack on the San Andreas Fault. Any suggestions?

A.—**Take up scuba diving and develop a taste for ABALONE.**

.

Q.—I have a near-complete collection of matchbooks. Besides collecting, is there any other use for matchbooks?

A.—**You could fix an awful lot of shaky table legs with them!**

.

Q.—My waterpipes freeze up every winter. Digging them up would mean destroying my strawberry patch. What am I to do?

A.—**You are a natural for a "Dairy Queen" franchise.**

.

Q.—I like outdoor cooking, but I live in a city eight-floor walk-up. Any suggestions?

A.—**Get a Hibachi, and heat your T.V. dinners on the fire escape.**

.

Q.—My wife has an electric clay kiln and I have an all electric power tool workshop. Together we blow all the fuses in the house.

A.—**One of the two of you... has to go on batteries!**

.

Q.—What does it take to tune up my car?

A.—**A very big B-flat tuning fork.**

Q.—My camper's septic system keeps over-flowing.
A.—**Keep driving downwind!**

•

Q.—Radar signals from planes keep opening my garage door.
A.—**Extend your driveway into an airstrip. There is a fortune to be made in stuck air travellers.**

•

Q.—Our swimming pool leaks into our garage, can you help us?
A.—**Indeed...park your car in the pool and swim in your garage!**

•

Q.—Where can I get spare parts for my 1962 SAAB?
A.—**From a junkyard in Uppsala, Sweden.**

•

Q.—Soldier Ants are marching toward my house!
A.—**Hire a tiny military band that's marching away from your house.**

•

Q.—How do I get rid of rust spots on garden furniture?
A.—**By staining the entire furniture "rust."**

Q.—Our roof leaks into our bedroom!
A.—Get a waterproof canopy bed.

•

Q.—How can I get more mileage out of my car?
A.—By pushing it!

•

Q.—When I do close work with my hammer and chisel, I always hit my head and break my glasses!
A.—Have your glasses bronzed.

•

Q.—I am using kitchen wastes to fertilize our herb garden. How come nothing grows?
A.—You are using inferior garbage!

•

Q.—What's the simplest way of installing a hidden sprinkler system on my lawn?
A.—Get together with your friendly local gopher.

•

Q.—I cure my own sauerkraut. My wife doesn't like the smell!
A.—Take daily showers and use an industrial deodorant.

Q.—Since 1956 I have been collecting string. I'd like to put it to some useful purpose now.

A.—Get two Dixie cups and call your mother more often.

•

Q.—On a recent trip I shot six rolls of film with my 35mm camera, but all the pictures came out with a mysterious blur on the left corner. What's wrong?

A.—Next time take your finger off the lens!

•

Q.—Can one clean a hot oven with turpentine?

A.—Yes, if you are tired of your face.

•

Q.—Building a new room divider, I walled up our telephone by mistake. Any suggestions?

A.—Let it ring.

•

Q.—The average weight of our family is 244 pounds. Is this too much strain on our living room floor?

A.—Not if you convert it into a sunken living room!

•

Q.—What's the cheapest way to burglar-proof my house?

A.—Drop marbles on your floors and put vaseline on all door knobs.

Q.—Planning to remodel my house I will need lots of powertools. Is it smarter to rent or to buy them?

A.—It's smartest to borrow them from your neighbor.

•

Q.—In ordering wood should I use the metric system?

A.—No, pick it up yourself or have it delivered.

•

Q.—I am a welder and have to go from work directly to a classy wedding. What shall I wear?

A.—A fireproof Tuxedo.

•

Q.—Is it all right to build a darkroom in our laundry?

A.—Yes, just don't put any starch in the negatives.

•

Q.—Will solar heat be enough to heat my 25-room home?

A.—Not if you live under a cloud.

INSTANT REPLAYS OF
SPORT GOOFS

INSTANT REPLAYS
OF SPORT GOOFS

INSTANT REPLAYS
OF SPORT GOOFS

INSTANT REPLAYS
OF SPORT GOOFS

INSTANT REPLAYS
OF SPORT GOOFS

INSTANT REPLAYS
OF SPORT GOOFS

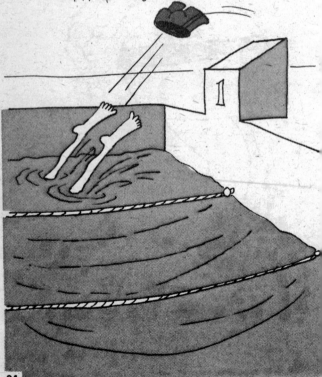

INSTANT REPLAYS
OF SPORT GOOFS

INSTANT REPLAYS
OF SPORT GOOFS

INSTANT REPLAYS
OF SPORT GOOFS

INSTANT REPLAYS OF SPORT GOOFS

INSTANT REPLAYS
OF SPORT GOOFS

INSTANT REPLAYS
OF SPORT GOOFS

INSTANT REPLAYS OF SPORT GOOFS

THE KLUTZ

A Klutz should not push a cork into a bottle with his thumb.

SELF-IMPROVEMENT HINTS

If you are too tall!

Wear baggy pants and slouch!

If you have bad breath!

Wear a nifty muffler!

If you are tense on the job!

Take short vacations!

If you are dull and boring!

Have your nose pierced and wear toe jewelry!

If you have unsightly dandruff!

Dress in fancy patterns!

If you have bad table manners!

Brown bag your meals!

If you are prematurely bald!

Cultivate long-haired friends!

If you have big hips!

Always remain seated!

If you are a bad sport!

Take up a solitary pastime!

If you have skinny legs!

Wear heavy hip boots!

THE KLUTZ

A Klutz should not stop his bicycle front brakes first.

HOW TO
INVITE TROUBLE
AND MAKE
THE WRONG CHOICE

Pick a pet....

That foams at the mouth.

Pick a landlord....

Who employs fulltime bodyguards.

Pick a roommate....

Who only owns one pair of socks.

Pick a disco partner....

Who wears constructionmen's boots.

Pick a blind date....

Whose idea of fun is wrestling gators.

Pick a dry cleaner....

Whose initials don't match the monogram on his shirt.

Pick a psychiatrist....

Who is hard of hearing.

Pick a car....

That comes with a warning from the Surgeon General.

Pick a political group....

That meets in cellars and whose members are masked.

Pick a waiter....

Who suffers from a bad head cold.

Pick a surgeon....

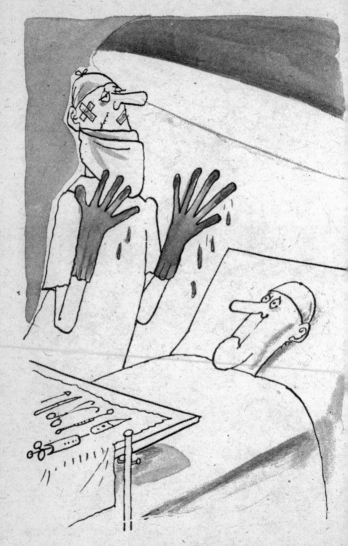

With cuts and nicks from shaving.

Pick an insurance company....

Whose main offices are in Citada di Rhumba, South America.

Pick an airline....

Whose pilots wear prescription goggles.

Pick a dentist....

With oversized hands.

Pick a hobby sport....

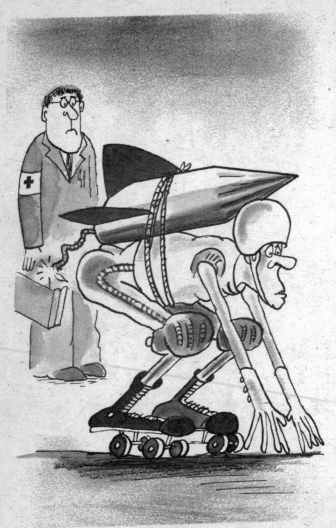

That needs an attending physician.

Pick a boyfriend....

Who wants you to meet his parole board.

Pick a girlfriend....

Who wears barbed wire curlers and opens bottles with her teeth.

Pick a resort spot....

That's off-limits to the Turkish armed forces.

Pick friends....

Who wear chains for belts and like to sit on people's faces.

MAD HOBBIES
FOR FUN AND PROFIT

For Profit...Worm farming.

For Fun...Hang gliding

For Profit... Traffic Spotter.

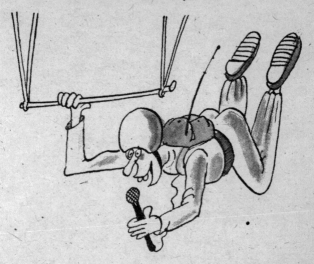

For Fun...Calligraphy.

For Profit... Envelope addressing.

For Fun...Cycling.

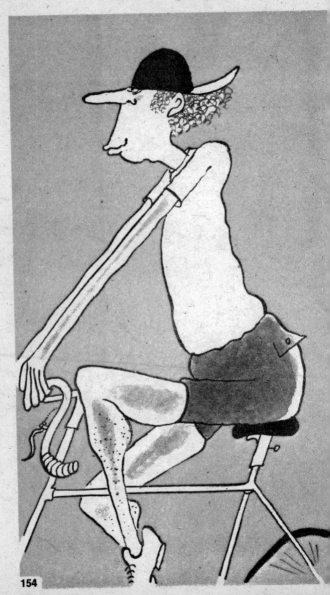

For Profit... Messenger service.

For Fun... Artistic hedge-trimming.

For Profit...Hair-styling.

For Fun... Butterfly mounting.

For Fun…Guitar-picking.

For Profit... Punk Rock Star performing.

THE KLUTZ

A Klutz should not trim hedges in a sculpture garden.

HOW NOT TO FIX IT!

How not to saw a plank down the middle.

How not to hang a birdfeeder.

How not to unplug a stopped-up sink.

How not to clean gutters.

How not to oil a hinge.

How not to plant a spring vegetable garden.

How not to spray-paint furniture.

How not to build a fireplace.

How not to put up wallpaper.

How not to insulate a house.

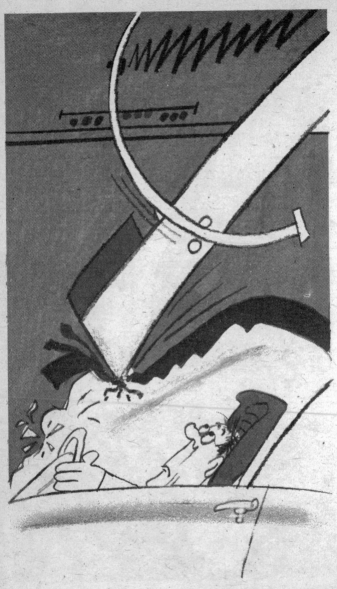

How not to install an automatic garage door opener.

THE MAD HOW **NOT** TO TOOL CHEST

Soft nails.

Non-retractable tape measure.

Over-ripe wood varnish.

Loose bottomed nail box.

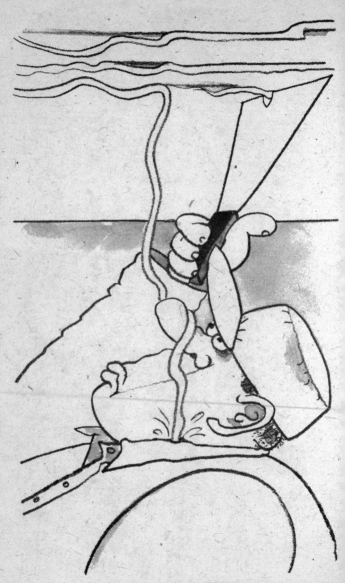

Dented plaster spatula.

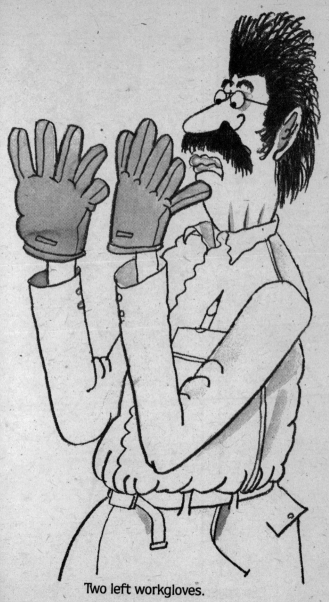

Two left workgloves.

Extra coarse paper in sander.

Flashlight with melt-down battery.

Unsheaved mat-cutting knife.

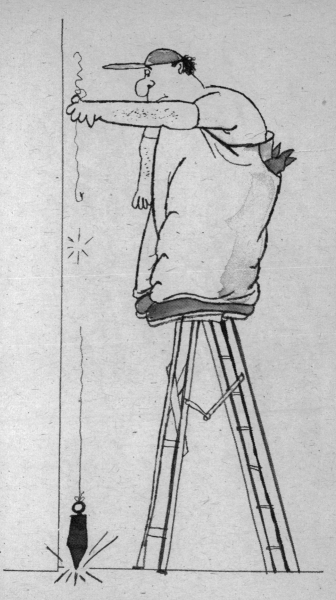

Loosely-knotted plumbline.

Leaky spraygun.

S-shaped ripsaw.

Mismatched nut and bolt.

Hammer with loose head.

Unadjustable welding torch.